GOODWOOD
COUNTRY
IN OLD PHOTOGRAPHS

One way to enjoy Goodwood country. A cyclist and his penny-farthing pose for the photographer. Mr L.R. Farley was a keen member of the Chichester Cycling Club in the 1880s, and his name is pencilled on the back of this portrait.

GOODWOOD COUNTRY
IN OLD PHOTOGRAPHS

COLLECTED BY

RICHARD PAILTHORPE & IAN SERRAILLIER

ALAN SUTTON
1987

Alan Sutton Publishing Limited
Brunswick Road · Gloucester

First published 1987

British Library Cataloguing in Publication Data

Goodwood country in old photographs.
1. Goodwood Region (West Sussex) — History
— Pictorial words 2. Goodwood Region
(West Sussex) — Description and travel —
Views
I. Pailthorpe, Richard   II. Serraillier, Ian
942.2'62   DA690.G6

ISBN 0-86299-356-3

THE COVER

A magnificent view of the Racecourse from the Trundle during the early 1900s. Between races a concert party and tipsters would perform on the course. Beyond the Grandstand was a fairground. The Grandstand, built in 1904 for £37,000, was demolished in 1979 and replaced by the present stand. It was built in time for the 1980 meeting at a cost of £3.6 million.

Typesetting and origination by
Alan Sutton Publishing Limited.
Printed in Great Britain
by Redwood Burn Limited

FOREWORD BY THE EARL OF MARCH

In 1697 when my ancestor, Charles Lennox, first Duke of Richmond, son of Charles II, bought a little hunting box called Goodwood, his purpose was to ride out with the Charlton Hunt, the first properly organised fox hunt in this country.

The Dukes of Grafton and St. Albans, also sons of Charles II, were members of the hunt, and the Duke of Monmouth, another son, hunted with them from time to time. Indeed, it was the hapless Monmouth who said 'When I am King I will hold my court at Charlton'. The hunt became so renowned that, we are told, 'Charlton pies were as famous as Melton Mowbray pies', whereas Goodwood then was as unknown to the world as Charlton is now.

As it did nearly three hundred years ago, Charlton lies within the Parish of Singleton and adjoins the Goodwood Estate. Today we still own several cottages in Singleton and Charlton, and a number of our employees and pensioners still live there.

For these particular reasons, I am delighted, as the tenth generation of the Lennox family, to write the foreword to this book about the pictorial history of the local villages. I know that the members of my own family and their descendants will be fascinated to gaze into the past, as will many others, and especially all the present and future residents of the area.

CONTENTS

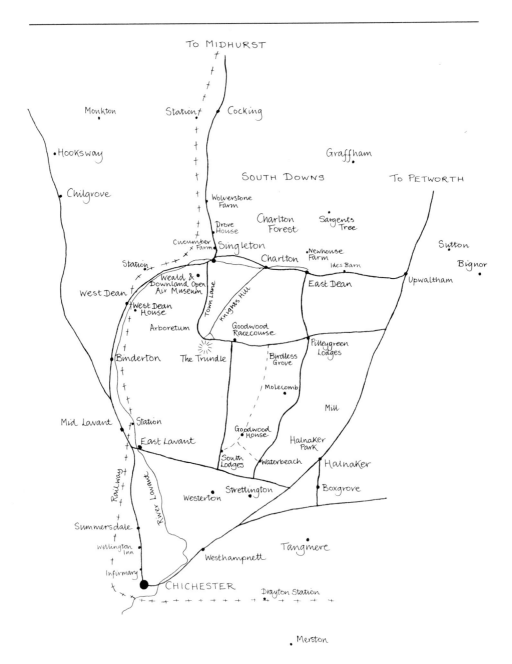

TO MIDHURST

Monkton

Station   Cocking

Hooksway

Graffham

SOUTH DOWNS

TO PETWORTH

Chilgrove

Wolverstone Farm

Charlton Forest

Sargents Tree

Sutton

Drove House

Cucumber Farm   Singleton

Newhouse Farm

Bignor

Station   Charlton

Ides Barn

Weald & Downland Open Air Museum

Upwaltham

West Dean

Town Lane

Knights Hill

East Dean

West Dean House

Arboretum

Goodwood Racecourse

Binderton

The Trundle

Birdless Grove

Pilleygreen Lodges

Molecomb

Mill

Mid Lavant   Station

East Lavant

Goodwood House

Halnaker Park

Railway

River Lavant

South Lodges   Waterbeach

Halnaker

Westerton   Strettington

Boxgrove

Summersdale

Wellington Inn

Tangmere

Infirmary

Westhampnett

CHICHESTER   Drayton Station

Merston

INTRODUCTION

This book is a photographic record of life in the Downland villages north of Chichester, particularly those in the Upper Lavant Valley and connected with the Goodwood and West Dean Estates. At the turn of the century the two Estates totalled over 28,000 acres, and between them they still own 18,000 acres today.

The photographs cover the last hundred years and concentrate on many aspects of country life. History does not stand still, and we have included some more recent photographs to illustrate changes and to show the development of the Weald and Downland Open Air Museum.

A number of the photographs were taken by the Revd Arthur Newman and his sister-in-law Mrs Jane Newman. Her husband, William, was vicar of East Dean and another Newman brother was vicar of Bignor and Sutton.

It has not been an easy task to select the photographs owing to the wealth of material available. We hope that we have been able to give readers some insight into life in this beautiful part of West Sussex.

Goodwood House *c.* 1900 with the Estate's shorthorn cows grazing in front. Built by the third Duke of Richmond at the end of the 18th century, it was designed by James Wyatt.

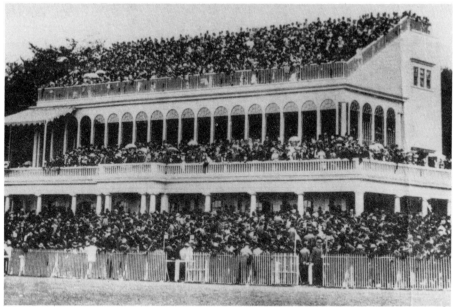

The Grandstand *c.* 1900. Racing had been started in 1801 by the third Duke of Richmond, who built the first stand, a timber-framed one. It was replaced by the fifth Duke in 1830 with this stand that could accommodate 3,000 people. The Royal Box is on the left with the canopy, overlooking the beech trees and lawn, so admired by Queen Alexandra. The stand was demolished in 1903.

SECTION ONE

Goodwood

Goodwood week at the end of July was by far the most important week of the year for the local villages, particularly Singleton. Memories of Race Week during its Edwardian heyday have been recorded, especially those of Mrs Grace Atkinson (née Miles) and the late Mr Jeff Farley.

Before 1914 Singleton was the focal point for almost everyone who had anything to do with horses. They flocked into the village – bookmakers, fruit stall and number board men, farriers, stable boys and trainers. They were called 'the Gentlemen', and were all put up in the village. To make way for them, the children sometimes had to sleep in the woodshed. Until 1905 Jeff Farley was usually sent away to stay with relations, as the trainers stayed in his parents' house. Among them were Mr Marsh the King's trainer, Mr Sam Darling and Mr Tom Jennings. Jeff remembers one of them, when he heard snores in his room, hauling a tramp from under the bed.

On the Sunday before Race Week, the cabs started to arrive from London. They stretched from the top of Budds Hill to well past Grove meadow. The tramps and tricksters arrived at the same time, and also half a dozen police. On Monday the horse specials arrived at Singleton station from Newmarket, Epsom, Lambourn, etc. Singleton and Charlton stabled about 75% of the runners.

On the first day of the races the village began to fill up from 6 a.m. onwards. Old Kate, a celebrated Cockney character, stood on the green triangle on the Charlton Road in her bonnet and black shawl, selling papers and race cards. Her language 'lit the morning air', as Grace Atkinson recalls. During the morning the race specials arrived at Singleton station. There was a barber's saloon outside the station, and anyone who wanted could have a haircut before stepping into a hansom. In Edwardian days most of the gentry went up to the course in carriages; there were plenty waiting at the station. They filled the village too, stretching all the way from Budds Hill to the bottom of Town Lane. On the steepest part of Town Lane people had sometimes to get out of their carriages and walk. Occasionally a carriage had to be given a tow. A spare horse was standing at the bottom of the lane in case it was needed.

The pubs had a man stationed by the Grove to run back and report when the crowds came pouring out of the station. Not everyone went up to the course by carriage, and many would stop for a drink before they began their walk up past the Church and over Lamb Down, or up the valley through Simmonds Dene. Boys and girls from the village took up their post at the gate behind the Church, holding out their caps and hats and singing:

Goodwood Races just begun,
You got money, we got none.
Now's the time to have some fun.
Up goes the donkey, down goes his tail!

They got quite a harvest, but pennies were hard to come by. They were not spent on sweets, but on boots for the winter. Perhaps it was because of Goodwood that Singleton children were better shod and dressed than children in other villages.

The Charlton Sawmill was closed during Race Week, so most of the men could get jobs either at Singleton or on the course. A popular job for boys was delivering telegrams for the Post Office. There was no direct telegraph line to the course – the Duke would not allow this. When the race was run, a man on the top of the Trundle signalled the result to the dewpond on Knight's Hill; it was passed on from there to the Sawmill, and from there to the papers. Another popular job for boys was clearing rubbish from the course before dawn, as well as picking up litter between races. A sovereign was the pay for a week's work.

At several points on the course the three card men and the Crown and Anchor men had their pitch, ready to run when a policeman arrived. On one occasion a policeman went up to the races dressed in civvies and found a three card gang operating behind the number board by the winning post. When he tried to arrest them, the gang set up a cry that he was a welshing bookmaker. The crowd took this up and chased him across the course. As he scrambled over the rails into the grandstand, someone broke a walking stick over his back. Later this policeman became Chief Constable of Reigate.

Tramps were a problem and slept anywhere – even with the pigs. But the barns and haystacks were their usual sleeping quarters. The police were issued with walking sticks to seek out the sleeping tramps. Any they found hanging about after the pubs closed were rounded up outside the Fox and Hounds. Then a sergeant counted them up and locked them in a stable for the night. Some of the tramps' names are still remembered – Starcross, Water Rat, Doncaster. Doncaster was a clever man who had come down in the world. They were real characters too, all of them. If the stable lads caught them, they ducked them in the river, then painted them with different colours of ochre – blue, red, yellow – when they came out. They didn't seem to mind.

Gypsies also came and were only allowed to camp on the side of Knight's Hill. They were not popular with foresters and gamekeepers, because they cut hazel to make clothes pegs which they put in old cocoa tins to sell to race-goers.

After the day's racing was over, there was plenty happening in the village. Jeff Farley's father used to get up a side, mostly of the Press, to play the jockeys at cricket, and prize fights took place in Simmonds Dene. Prize fighting was illegal and had to be arranged in secrecy. A fight between two boxers, Billy Camp and George Abbott, was organised at East Dean by 'Squire' George Alexander Baird, a one-time admirer of Lily Langtry. Billy Camp was disguised as Baird's coachman. The ring was mowed on Astead Down and horse shoes nailed on to gate posts showed the way. The fight was to take place very early in the morning but the police got wind of it and tried to surround the ring. They arrested one of the seconds, but both fighters got away and raced down to Ides Barn. They hid under the hay and were not discovered by the authorities, though the shepherd got a rare shock when he went to the barn and saw a pair of eyes looking at him out of the hay!

In the evening after dinner the concert party, which the trainers used to hire to play on the course between races, came along and played on the Farleys' lawn — they managed a crowd of two or three hundred in the road outside as well. King Edward VII's horses were always stabled with the Farleys and in 1896 he came round in the evening to see them. That was also the year that Lily Langtry stayed in the village and King Edward was seen having tea with her in the garden.

Such was racing week in the old days. When it was over, 'the Gentlemen' went away, but they left their fleas behind them! Motor transport gradually increased up to 1914 and after the First World War the number of racegoers and horse specials declined. The closure of the Station to passengers in 1935 marked the end of an era for Singleton.

Duke of Richmond. Rt. Hon. Henry Chaplin. Late Lord Henry Gordon-Lennox. Marchioness of Blandford. Earl of Sandwich. Lord Algernon Gordon-Lennox. Sir Fredk. Johnstone. Late Earl Annesley. Hon. W. Carrington.

The late Earl of Bradford. H.M. The King. Countess of Lucan. H.M. Queen Alexandra. Duchess of Buccleuch. Lady Constance Howard. Lady Caroline Gordon-Lennox.

A Goodwood House Party in 1866 with Edward, then Prince of Wales, sitting second from the right and the future seventh Duke of Richmond behind him. Princess Alexandra is sitting in the centre.

A Goodwood House Party in 1907. King Edward VII is in the centre with the seventh Duke of Richmond and Prince George, later King George V, standing behind. Mrs Keppel, Edward's last recognised mistress, is third from the left.

King Edward VII in 1906 leaving Goodwood House for the Races.

King Edward VII in 1907 leaving for the Races with Prince George in a Fiat car.

King Edward VII and Prince George arriving at the Racecourse. The seventh Duke of Richmond can just be identified behind the King.

Carriages passing Goodwood House *c.* 1900 *en route* for the Racecourse via the Birdless Grove.

The Revd Arthur Newman in the Birdless Grove. The Grove was so called because of its stillness, unbroken even by birdsong.

Stable lads at Manor Farm, East Lavant, some time during the late 19th century. The tenant farmer Isaac Walters ran a training stable for racehorses. Standing left to right are the trainer, with whip and stop watch; the farrier; the saddle boy; the assistant farrier with toolbox; the harness lad; the man with the pitchfork for cleaning out. Sitting left to right are two further lads and a boy with a plate.

The Grandstand enclosure c. 1900. The ladies are wearing the fashions of the day while the men wear hats, some of them boaters. King Edward VII had a great influence on male fashions. After 1906 the traditional top hat and tails were gradually replaced by more informal dress and panama hats.

The start of the Goodwood Cup in 1920. The race has traditionally been started from the 'Trundle End' and was won by Mount Royal, a bay colt owned by Lady Cunliffe-Owen. Ridden by Steve Donoghue, he won by three lengths.

The Grandstand enclosure and paddock c. 1900. In the background is the Iron Age fort, known as the Trundle or St Roches Hill, a popular place open to all until it was enclosed in 1929.

The same view shortly after the Second World War. Attendance after the war increased dramatically, reaching a record in 1953, when 62,000 people watched from the Trundle during the four day meeting.

Described by King Edward VII as 'a garden party with racing tacked on', the same atmosphere of enjoyment has always prevailed.

Race traffic making its way up Trundle Hill for the 1925 meeting.

The view from the Trundle during a meeting in the 1920s.

Goodwood Park. The third Duke of Richmond planted the cedar trees during the second half of the 18th century. During the 19th century the West Sussex Agricultural Society held an annual sheep shearing competition under the trees. The photograph is taken from the site of the present cricket field, although 'the square' in the picture appears to be in the wrong position. James Lillywhite, who captained England in the first ever series against Australia in 1876–77, lived at Westerton and played cricket for Goodwood.

The Shell House, Goodwood park. It was built as a grotto during the 1730s by Sarah, the second Duchess of Richmond and her daughters. It took seven years to complete, the shells coming from many parts of the world. In the early part of this century when this photograph was taken it was open to the public. Unfortunately many shells were removed by visitors, and one-fifth had to be replaced.

Pilleygreen Lodges, built by the third Duke of Richmond in 1794. Both lodges and coach houses have particularly fine flintwork. The origin of the name Pilleygreen is uncertain, but the siting of the lodges was part of the Duke's uncompleted plan to enclose the park.

The Chichester or South Lodges, designed by James Wyatt. The lodge-keeper would live in one lodge and sleep in the other.

Waterbeach Lodge at the eastern entrance to the park, so-called because in prehistoric times this was the point where the sea once reached.

The last meet of the Goodwood Hunt, on 13 April 1895 outside Molecomb House. It had been re-established in 1883, but by 1895 for reasons of economy it was disbanded.

Molecomb Cottages. Molecomb was designed by James Wyatt as the Dower House to Goodwood in about 1800. The present Duke of Richmond, who lived there from 1904 until 1928, remembers the names of the occupants of the cottages. Nearest to the House was George Wackford, the gardener. He also operated the Drake and Gorham oil engine that drove the dynamo for the 50 volt house electric system. Next was Mr Marshall, the butler; then Mr Johnson, the groom. Mr Kennett, who worked at the Home Farm sawmill, lived in the end cottage. On his way to work and back over Hat Hill he trod steps, good and deep, into the turf. These were visible for years after and known as 'Kennett's Steps'. His diminutive wife wore one of his caps secured by a very long and protruding hat pin. The cottages and doorstep of Molecomb House are in East Dean parish, and the main part of the House in Singleton Parish.

The Duke of Richmond's private airfield, in the field near the South Lodges. It was used by the Duke during the late 1930s, before the present airfield, later the Motor Circuit, was established during the Second World War. The thatched hangar was latterly used as a wood turnery and burnt down in 1954. The twin-engined aircraft was built by the Duke and a friend, Edmund Hordern, at Heston. The Duke remembers an amusing incident. Worried by the danger to intruding members of the public, a notice saying 'Private Mushrooms Cultivated' was erected. No sooner had this happened than he found a group of people with baskets busily searching the field. They could only be dispersed by flying over them at almost ground level. They lay flat and very soon departed!

West Dean

West Dean House with its 8,500 acre Estate was bought by Mr Willie James in 1891. His wife Evelyn became one of Edwardian Society's best known hostesses. During the 1890s and the first decade of this century Edward Prince of Wales, later King Edward VII, was a frequent visitor. Other royal visitors included Queen Alexandra, the future King George V and Queen Mary, and King Alfonso XIII of Spain. These royal visits were a mark of high honour. It was then most unusual for a Queen consort to sleep in the home of a commoner. The poet Hilaire Belloc composed the following few lines about these famous parties:

> * There will be bridge and booze till after three,
> And after that, a lot of them will grope
> Along the corridors in *robes de nuit*,
> Pyjamas, or some other kind of dope.
> A sturdy matron will be set to cope,
> With Lord ———, who isn't "quite the thing",
> And give his wife the leisure to elope,
> And Mrs. James will entertain the King!

Mr Willie James died in 1912 and the Estate was held in Trust until their son Edward (1907–1984) came of age. He was an art collector and a major patron of the surrealists. After the Second World War he spent much of his time abroad, living principally in Mexico. In 1964 he established the Edward James Foundation as a charitable educational Trust, and the House became a College specialising in residential courses for teaching arts and crafts.

*   By courtesy of A.D. Peters and Co. Ltd. on behalf of the estate of Hilaire Belloc.

A shooting party outside the Norwegian Hut in the Arboretum. It was brought back from Norway by Mr Willie James in his yacht the '*Lancashire Witch*.' Here the ladies would join the gentlemen for lunch, and it was common practice for a photograph to be taken. King Edward VII, characteristically smoking a cigar, is standing with Mrs James (centre). Willie James is at the bottom of the steps to the right of the railpost.

King Edward VII shooting on the West Dean Estate. The Visitors Book records that 'excellent sport was obtained by the Royal Party – with the King shooting very well, bringing down his birds "left and right." '

Shooting in West Dean Park. Bags of 1000 pheasants a day were common during the November House Parties. King Edward would leave the House at 10.45 a.m. and return at 4.15 p.m., with the usual break for lunch in the middle of the day. Lunch consisted of 'plenty of hot dishes and an invigorating soup', and there would be champagne and whisky to drink. It would probably be brought to the Arboretum or to a barn, scrupulously cleaned out for the occasion. While the gentlemen were out shooting, the ladies would spend the time visiting local places of interest such as the Cowdray Ruins at Midhurst or Chichester Cathedral.

King Alfonso XIII King of Spain (1886–1931) and grandfather of the present King Juan Carlos. He stayed at West Dean from 11–16 November 1907, with his wife Queen Eugenie and her mother Princess Henry of Battenberg, who had arrived by motor car and not by the customary train. The young couple had survived an assassination attempt on their wedding day a year earlier. The King was very keen on shooting. During his stay a band played every evening in the corridor outside the dining room, and the grounds were illuminated.

Gamekeepers after a tea break in the Warren, West Dean. From the Middle Ages until the early 19th century, West Dean had a 900 acre Rabbit Warren. Unlike today, rabbits were not considered vermin and were kept by landowners for their meat and fur. The trugs held by the keepers were used for carrying the game feed.

West Dean House Staff during the early 1900s. The house-keeper is sitting in the middle of the front row.

The funeral procession of Mr Willie James in 1912.

Edward James (centre) and his wife Tilly Losch (to his left) with some of the cast of 'Les Ballets' at West Dean in 1933. The ballet was designed for Tilly Losch by Georges Balanchine and financed by Edward. It ran for a season at the Théatre des Champs Elysées in Paris and also at the London Savoy. For a short time during the early 1930s when Edward took up residence in the House it was once again used for entertaining. Artists and poets such as Rex Whistler, John Betjeman and the photographer Cecil Beaton were regular guests. Edward's marriage to Tilly Losch lasted for three years and ended in 1936.

Monkton House built in 1902–3 by Lutyens for the James's as a shooting box and family retreat from West Dean. It was also sometimes used as a place for the children to stay during house parties.

Monkton House after Edward James's 'surrealist' alterations of 1936 onwards. Christopher Nicholson and his assistant Hugh Casson were commissioned as architects, while Norris Wakefield undertook interior work. The palm trees are made of fibreglass and wooden sheets were added below the windows to look like linen airing.

The entrance door with two palm trees that were carved by an Austrian father and son, misleadingly named 'English'. They also carried out work inside West Dean House.

Edward James's bedroom. The design of the four poster bed was based on Nelson's or Napoleon's funeral hearse.

Binderton House in 1892 when Mr and Mrs James held a Goodwood week house party there, while alterations were being carried out to West Dean House. Binderton was built by William Smith in about 1680 and further alterations were made in the 18th century. In the 1940s and early 1950s it was the country home of the former Prime Minister, Sir Anthony Eden.

The Villages

A number of the villages are in the Upper Lavant Valley. The River Lavant is not much more than a seasonal stream, taking its name from the word 'Levant' or 'Lavant' meaning land-spring. Traditionally, the springs break out at East Dean in mid-February or earlier during a wet winter.

The stream begins as a water course alongside the road between East Dean and Charlton. On reaching Singleton it is joined by another spring, from a small swampy field called the 'Hop Garden' near Cucumber Farm. It then continues its eleven mile journey round Chichester and into the Harbour near Dell Quay.

At the time of the Domesday Book it was able to turn two mills at Singleton and another at Lavant. During the 19th century it was also used to irrigate four or five hundred acres, which in summer provided two or three tons of hay per acre. The remains of the sluices and channels, used also for damming the river for sheep-washing, can still be seen between Singleton and West Dean.

Mid Lavant. Looking south on the Chichester road. James Wheale's grocery shop is on the right with a well head in front.

Mid Lavant. A view of East Lavant. The village was described by Dallaway as 'pleasantly situated on small eminences, falling in every direction to the rivulet Lavant, which is particularly broad and shallow'.

East Lavant. Men chatting by the Sheepwash. It was here that the sheep waded out of the river after being washed. The man on the left is holding a stone jar flagon and the one opposite him seems to be having a drink.

East Lavant. Drovers. The cottage was badly damaged by fire in 1935, but later restored. Note the small roof of the privy at the end of the garden. In the background to the left of the cottage can be seen part of a 'Duchess Cottage' which was the schoolmaster's house.

East Lavant. School Group in 1903. The headmaster, Mr A.J. Woodman, is on the right. He was headmaster from 1884 until 1905, when he died after falling off his bicycle in Pook Lane and fracturing his skull.

East Lavant. Lady Gifford's Harriers meeting in front of the Green on Boxing Day, 1910. The Harriers came from Bosham.

East Lavant. Woodman's Stores. The proprietor Mr S. Woodman was the son of the schoolmaster, Mr A. J. Woodman. He had a large assortment of sweets, tobacco and cigarettes. Minerals for sale included ginger beer and lemonade, costing a penny a bottle.

East Lavant. Football Team by the Memorial Hall 1921. Back Row: Mr Holdaway (station master), S. 'Putty' Bridle, W. Ide, B. Squires, Mr Brodie, Kruger Chalk, J. Clements, C. Foster, Mr Melling (landlord of The Royal Oak). Front Row: C. 'Bustler' Horn, R. Fielder, F. Southern, R. MacArthy, G. Southern.

The Home Guard being inspected outside West Dean House by Colonel Willis and Captain Emery. In the front row are Privates Budd, Brown, Haytor; Sergeant Foster; Privates Squires, Puttick and Goodchild.

Maurice Carter at work in the forge. Maurice's father, James Carter, moved from West Dean in 1901 to take over the Chilgrove Forge. Maurice joined his father as a blacksmith in 1924 and retired in 1980. The inter-war years were the last great days of the heavy horse. The Carters looked after all the horses on neighbouring farms, as well as repairing agricultural machinery and tyring cart wheels.

The Forge in 1889. The same grindstone was used by the Carters for sharpening implements such as axes, scythes and billhooks. The pond has long been dry, but was an important source of water when tyring a cart wheel.

Chilgrove Manor. The house was the home of the Woods Family and sometimes visited by Gilbert White, the Selborne naturalist. It was demolished in 1853, and its replacement has recently been converted into apartments.

Hooksway. Alf and Carrie Ainger outside the Royal Oak. Alf was landlord from 1907 until 1971, during which time he and the pub became part of the local folklore. His many reminiscences included a visit from King Edward VII while out shooting on the West Dean Estate. He is probably best known for the reply he gave to the Midhurst licensing magistrate when asked what toilet facilities were available – 'I got nine acres, sir.'

West Dean School, infants' class, c. 1923. Their teacher Mrs Veale, the headmaster's wife, is second on the left in the back row. Next to her are the two Mitchell boys – called Shaver (because of his close-cropped hair) and Shirty (because his shirt tail was always hanging out). Mr and Mrs Veale were strict but much liked by their pupils. There were no school meals in those days. Children brought their own sandwiches with them, and for a drink they cupped their hands under the tap in the cloakroom. In the lunch hour they could wander off into the fields, blackberrying etc., but had to be punctual for afternoon school, which ended at 3 p.m.

Bill and Dolly Boxall in the playground of West Dean School before World War 1. They were the 24th and 25th in a family of 27.

The village street early this century.

The mill pond and watermill to the right.

Mrs West standing outside her cottage, at the back of Mr Lambert's the coal merchant.

Cocking school and war memorial. The old toll house, now demolished, is on the left.

The Causeway, early this century, looking towards Midhurst.

The School in 1901. John Farley is second from the right in the third row from the front. John was born in the Bell Inn, where his father was landlord. The family moved to Wolverstone Farm on the Singleton road, where John and his younger brother William ran the farm until John's retirement in 1970. A new village school was built in 1967 and the old school building was converted into flats.

View of the crossroads, looking towards Levin Down. Its clump of trees was planted by Napoleonic Prisoners of War. Pennicotts' Shop is on the right.

Horse and cart on the bridge by the pond, early in the century.

Bay Cottage, now Little Garth, c. 1900. It had bay trees either side of the door, and pear and peach trees growing up the wall.

Cobblers or Middle Row c. 1900. Mr. Smith, who died in 1973 aged 97, lived in the left hand end cottage. His mother (in white dress) is standing in front of the creeper. Other occupants of the Row included (left to right), Mr Croucher who worked at Charlton Sawmill; Mr Clarke who worked at the Sawmill; Mr Dorman, the Station signalman; Mr Bulbeck, the unofficial pig killer; Mr Elliot, a bricklayer on the West Dean Estate; and Mr. West, who also worked at the Sawmill.

The girl in white by the flint wall is probably Clare or Florrie Ticehurst. The cottages behind her have now been replaced by modern houses. The top building on the right is the Old Rectory.

Little Yarne and number 6, Singleton. On the far left is the corner of a flint stable, now the village surgery, which the Summersdale doctors visit twice a week for surgeries.

Old Cottages, by the grass triangle on the Charlton road. It was here that Old Kate sold race cards during Goodwood week. Levin Down with its clump of trees is on the far right.

The Horse and Groom Inn early in the century. Henry Westbrook, the village decorator, stands fifth from the left. He always wore a bowler hat wherever he went.

The well at St Francis Cottage, c. 1909. Noah Hoad (seated), village carpenter, coffin maker and odd jobs man, shared the well with Mrs Arthur Smith (second from right), who lived in the front cottage. Cissie Hoad, Noah's daughter, is standing (far left) and Mrs Elizabeth Miles (far right).

The Saxon Church in 1893, photographed by two young photographers from Westbourne.

A race crowd or possibly a wedding gathering, photographed on Singleton bridge by two Westbourne photographers in 1893. Mr Alick Farley, the churnmaker and father of Jeff, lived in the house on the right. His stables, now Pearman's Garage, were behind.

The two photographers with their plate camera. They worked in the boot trade and photography was their hobby.

The 'Religious Bookshop'. Here Mrs Targett sold hymn books, psalm books and religious tracts. Has the boy outside come to buy something? In his straw hat, white Eton collar and dark suit, he seems most suitably dressed. William Staples, father of Tom the builder, lived in the house on the left.

Mrs 'Widow' Targett seated outside her home, the Religious Bookshop.

Group Two of the school in 1913, with their teacher Miss Grey, a gardener's daughter. Next to her is Olive Jack, who married Stanley Brown of Manor Farm. The girl in the middle of the front row holding the Group Two slate board is Evelyn Holden, the policeman's elder daughter.

The Cricket Team early this century.

The Football Team early this century. Back row: G. Pearce (groundsman), G. Long, A. Witham, C. Pratt, J. Frogbrook, W. Baker, A. Lovelock, J. Burningham (Secretary). Front row: W. Mant, C. Wood, R. Jones, W. Sopp, J. Schoefield.

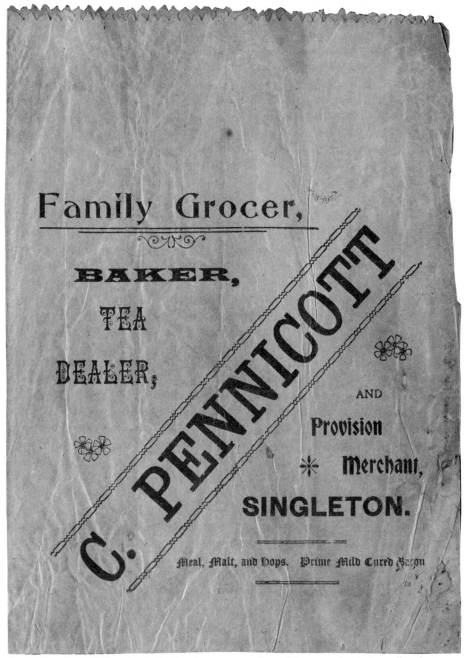

Paper Bag from C. Pennicott, the family grocer and provision merchant. As well as being a baker and tea dealer he sold meal, malt, hops and prime, mild-cured bacon.

Postcard to Mrs C. Gumbleton, East Dean, from a soldier in D. Company, 4th Royal Sussex Regiment, trenching at Arundel Camp, 1912. 'I am sending a card from us at camp . . . not very hard work. Arthur.'

Members of Singleton and East Dean Women's Institute planting potatoes on Lamb Down. They are Mrs Norrell, Mrs Phillips, Mrs Eade, Mrs Dyer and Mrs Hoad, 1915.

Mrs Norrell and Mrs Eade earthing up potatoes. Levin Down can be seen in the background.

Peace celebrations, 1919, in the recreation field. The milk churn on the left was made by Mr Alick Farley. Every day Albert Chalk drove a milk cart full of churns of milk like this one to Singleton station, to catch the Chichester train.

Drove House, a former hunting lodge owned by Lord Leconfield at the end of the 19th century. Part of the house was once an Inn known as the Drovers Arms. The main road then passed close to it and was diverted when the house was enlarged by the Egremont family in the 18th century. It was reputedly a haunt of smugglers and used for the storage of contraband.

The Paragon Excursion Car outing, c. 1920. Passengers from Singleton include Beatrice Farley (second from left, top row), her mother Mary (in front of her, dark hat), and her bank manager father Percy is there too.

Charlie Wells feeding his geese in the field by his cottage. He lost his right arm in the First World War.

The Wellington Inn, situated on the Broyle Road to the north of Chichester in about 1907. Charlie Wells is the small boy sitting on the gate with his cricket bat. Charlie's uncle, Ted Whitney, the licensee is on the left bringing out the beer. Next to him is George Whitney. The two girls in front are Rose and Florrie Whitney. Mrs Whitney is looking out from the door on the right. In 1747 a gang of smugglers assembled in Charlton Forest to plan a raid on Poole Customs House. A stone opposite the Inn marks the spot where some of the gang were hanged two years later for their crimes including murder.

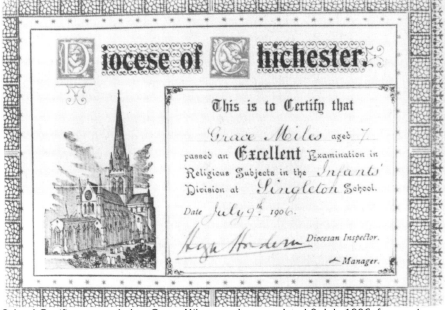

School Certificate awarded to Grace Miles, aged seven, dated 9 July 1906, for passing an Excellent examination in the Infants' Division of the school. It is signed by Hugh Hordern, the vicar of Singleton, who later became Bishop of Lewes.

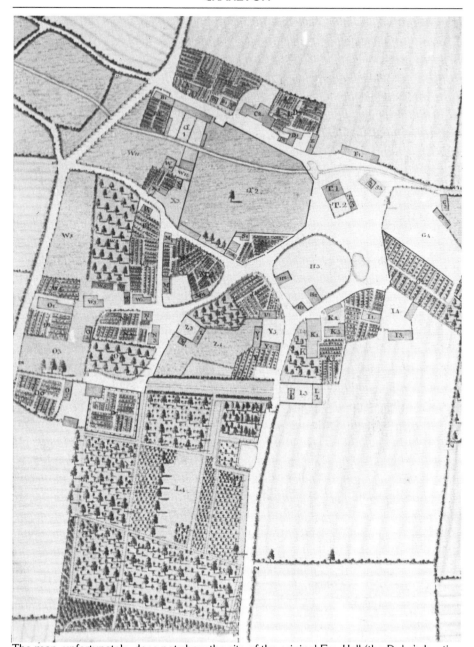

The map, unfortunately, does not show the site of the original Fox Hall (the Duke's hunting Lodge was renamed Fox Hall at a later date). The Hall was designed by Burlington for the Huntsmen's evening entertainment. It was used as a banqueting room, saloon, concert room, drawing room, assembly and ballroom. In front it had a flagstaff, and on the top a weathercock in the form of a gilded fox.

Fox Hall during the 1880s when Thomas Foster, manager of Charlton Sawmill, lived here. It had been built by the second Duke of Richmond in 1731 as his hunting lodge. The architects were Lord Burlington and possibly Roger Morris, who was later to design Carnés Seat in Goodwood Park.

Fox Hall is now owned by the Landmark Trust. They have restored it to suggest its 18th century grandeur and now let it as holiday accommodation.

William Laishley standing outside the Fox. He became landlord in 1903. The Inn dates from the 16th century and played a prominent part during the heyday of the Charlton Hunt. The village bakery was through the closed door, adjoining the road. A plaque on the wall inside records that the first Women's Institute to be formed in England met here on 9 November 1915. Singleton and East Dean W.I. continues to flourish.

Mrs Nora Laishley serving Arch Long in the Fox. Mrs Laishley came to the Fox when she married Mr Philip Laishley in 1937, and she was licensee from 1957 until 1985. Arch's first visit to the Fox was in 1915 when he and other children from East Dean School performed a play 'The Magic Spinning Wheel' in the clubroom.

A view looking towards Fox Hall in the distance, taken from the farm early this century.

Leonard or Albert Aylwin outside Charlton Farm buildings, now the craft workshops and stores of the Weald and Downland Open Air Museum. During the 1920s there were 14 horses on the farm looked after by four horsemen, who had to get up at 4.30 a.m. – earlier than the other farm workers – to prepare their horses for the day ahead. Work finished at 5 p.m. – but then at the end of the long day the horsemen still had to 'rack up' – seeing that their horses were fed and groomed.

Leonard or Albert Aylwin standing outside Charlton Farmhouse. Leonard, Albert, William and Henry Aylwin together with their sisters Rose, May and Annie took over the running of Charlton Farm in 1913. The house was once the hunting lodge of the Duke of Devonshire and Lord Harcourt. The Farm remained in the Aylwin family until 1968 when Joe Aylwin, who had taken on the tenancy from his uncles, retired.

Mr Dyer the postman outside his house in Charlton. The letters were delivered from Chichester by horse and cart, arriving at 8.30 a.m. and 4 p.m. The wall letterbox had two collections on weekdays at 9.30 a.m. and 6.30 p.m., and on Sundays one at 11.25 a.m.

Boys playing marbles in 1893 by the farm. 'Small ring' was the usual game, although 'big ring' would be played when it was possible to find a smooth piece of ground. Other terms used were 'clears levelance,' meaning permission to smooth a piece of ground, and the cry of 'no pooks' or 'no bunnocks' was raised when the toll (the marble used for shooting) was not shot cleanly.

Mr Osborne, who worked at the Sawmill, sitting outside his cottage. He is wearing corduroy trousers and a moleskin waistcoat.

Mrs Phoebe Miles standing outside Fox Hall.

Post Office Row and the Star and Garter on the far right, with Mrs Lambert at the door. The end cottage on the right, No. 9, was the Post Office from 1891–1942. Mrs White, who lived to be 102 years old, stands in the door. She was post-mistress until 1921, when the P.O. was taken over by Mr Horace Austin.

These three cottages were built by the Goodwood Estate to replace some of the nine cottages and four or five barns destroyed by fire on 24 April 1852. They stand at right angles to the road because the sixth Duchess of Richmond said 'they must face south'. Mrs Gumbleton stands outside the cottage (left) and the Poling family (right).

Cleaning out the pond with dung carts in 1905. This was a 'goodwill job' done by the farmer and volunteers during the summer when the pond was at its lowest. The man in the foreground is Mr B. West.

The job still has to be done today – local farmer David Humphrey assists with his JCB.

The Mud Pond, now filled in and the site of a bus shelter. A timber framed pig-sty and bee skeps can just be seen in the garden, with the church in the background.

The village baker delivering bread in Butcher's Lane to Mrs Reeves, Mrs Osborne and Mrs West. The two boys are Ernie and Reg Osborne.

Mrs West, Mrs Reeves and Mrs Osborne outside their cottages in Butcher's Lane, so called because (we are told) the inhabitants were always peering out at passers-by. At the far end is Mr Reeves the carrier with his horse and cart. Note also the bird cages on the cottage walls.

Village girls lined up in front of the pond.

The Shop in 1912. The shop-keeper Mr Saunders is standing outside with his daughter Ivy and the three Chisell girls. He had a girl assistant who was very popular with the village boys. Notices outside advertise White Rose American Lamp Oil, Epps Cocoa, and 'One and all manures and seeds'. In the windows are meat carcases, calico rolls, saucepans, teapots, crockery, and hobnail boots at 5s.11d a pair. The board on the left announces the best buy of the day – 'Finest Figs 4d the pound'. The three bicycles outside belong to girls. When they left school they usually went into service and could soon afford to buy one of these quite cheaply second-hand.

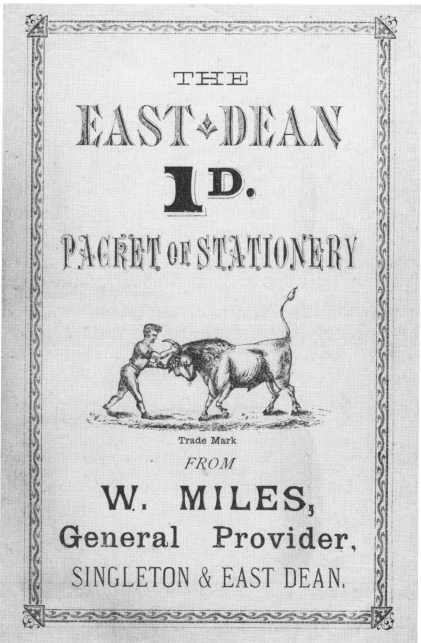

The East Dean 1*d* packet of stationery from W. Miles.

The pond on a postcard stamped and dated 19 September 1908.

The message reads: 'Dear Topsy
Just a p.c. in answer to yours as I thought you would not think about me when you got away. Do you know we are going away a month's notice last Saturday Alf and all of us it is a shame after so many years and I shall miss going away from all my friends, you and Edie and Bet. My A. is coming down Saturday for a week so I shall be landed next week old dear hope you enjoying your holiday. With love from your friend Emily.'

The Chapel on the left was built in 1902.

East Dean Band early in the century. Back row: H. Lillywhite, Charlie Johnson, G. Waymark, G. Switzer, Harry Gumbleton. Front row: Bill Gumbleton, Charles Waymark, Walter Read, Charlie Phillips. They played at all the functions in the villages.

East Dean Band in the garden of Sutton Vicarage. On the left the vicar Revd Newman is talking to the bandmaster.

East Dean Football team, 1925. Back row: N. Budgen, R. Croucher, V. Lambert, E. Austen, H. Austen, R. Mitchell. Front row: P. Stevens, C. Croucher, H. Passmore, W. Croucher, G. Budd.

The Pride of the Village. School Group in 1912.

School Group c. 1925. Miss Smith, nicknamed 'Miff-Miff', is on the right.

The Bonfire on the Green in preparation for Guy Fawkes Night c. 1950. The children (left to right) are: A. Miles, B. Merry, I. Stevens, D. Hammond, L. Pearce, C. Mills, M. Dempsey and H. Stevens.

Revd W. Newman, vicar of East Dean and rector of Upwaltham 1895–1919, with three friends in the field at the bottom of the vicarage garden.

Revd Newman with his goats. Gardening and looking after his animals – he also kept hens, chickens and pigs – were his hobbies. He had a boy to help him, but did most of the work himself. His wife Jane is on the left.

Jane Newman in the vicarage garden dressed as a milk-maid. She was very keen on amateur theatricals, organised them and made many of the costumes herself. She was also an accomplished photographer and took a number of the photographs in this book, together with her brother-in-law, the Revd Arthur Newman.

Robert Browning's poem 'The Pied Piper of Hamelin' performed in the vicarage garden. Charles Remnant, who was living in the village at the time, was the pied piper. The children were from the village school.

Mr and Mrs Kennett.

The Newman family picnicking near Amberley.

Captain Sargent's Tree

This is high up in Charlton Forest and very difficult to find. 'An atrocious murder' was committed here in 1807. George Sargent was a Captain in the 9th Regiment of Foot. He was taken prisoner in the French War, but he escaped and returned to Lavington where he lived. On 7 November he set out from Graffham with some gentlemen and farmers to find a highwayman who was hiding in the forest. The highwayman was a Graffham man, James Allan or Ayling, a deserter from Captain Sargent's own Regiment. Captain Sargent, who was better mounted than his companions, outstripped them and was the first to come up with the highwayman, who shot him dead just by this beech tree, now known as Captain Sargent's Tree. The highwayman eluded his pursuers for a week. But then a farmer out hunting duck heard something stirring in a pond. He fired his gun and shot the highwayman.

That is the story as it is told by A.W. Wilberforce in 1919 in 'A History of a Sussex Family'. There is however another version:

The highwayman used to hold up travellers regularly on the Bury road. All this time he hid in Charlton Forest, in what is now known as Allan's Ditch. His sister used to bring him food secretly from Graffham and one day she was followed. When Allan heard his pursuers coming he hid in a pond or a stream, submerging himself in the water and breathing through a straw, but his pursuer saw him and shot him as he lay there.

Mr Arch Long saved the beech tree from being felled during the 1930s. He is seen in the picture standing in front of the tree.

Boxgrove Priory with the ruins of the medieval monastic guest house in the foreground. The Benedictine Priory was in 1537 a victim of King Henry VII's dissolution of the monasteries, leaving only the Priory Church for the villagers to worship in. In 1622 six parishioners were prosecuted for playing cricket in the churchyard on a Sunday.

The old vicarage c. 1900. The gentleman with the dogs is possibly the Revd Edward Hill, vicar from 1891–1911. The vicarage occupied the present site of Priory Gate House and was demolished during the late 1930s.

The village street during the early 1900s.

The Boys' School, founded by the Countess of Derby in 1741 as a hospital for 'twelve old women' and a school for 18 children from the parishes of Boxgrove, East Lavant and Tangmere. It is now almshouses for elderly people.

Football Team 1912. The team were nicknamed the Canaries and played in Halnaker Park. The players were A. Glasspool, J. Whittle, W. White, J. Abbott, G. Glasspool, H. Parvin, B. Treagus, N. Salisbury, S. Leggatt, S. Passmore, C. Blunden.

The ruins of Halnaker House, a medieval fortified mansion with Tudor additions. During the 16th century it was the home of Thomas West, Lord de la Warr, and was visited by King Edward VI on 27 July 1551. One of its interesting features was a well house with a 219 foot well, operated by a donkey wheel. The House had become part of the Goodwood Estate in 1765, after which it gradually fell into disrepair.

Halnaker Park. The cottages and adjoining farmstead occupied the site of what was probably the Home Farm to Halnaker House.

The village shop on the right belonged to F. Pennicott, whose family also ran the Singleton Shop. The thatched cottage was badly damaged by fire during the 1930s and later demolished. Blunden's fuel yard and the village bakery, both just out of the picture, were sited at the crossroads.

Mr Sawyer, the village blacksmith and farrier, stands outside the forge. It is still in use today.

A loaded wagon of bavins outside the Anglesey Arms. The bavins were probably being delivered to Blunden's, the village fuel merchants. The empty wagon appears to be on its way to collect a similar load, and the two drivers have obviously stopped for refreshment.

Harry Parker, the landlord's son, outside the Anglesey Arms. The family supplied milk to the village and kept a small herd of Jersey cows. These were milked in the outbuildings, now demolished, in the background.

Stane Street, the old Roman Road from Chichester to London, goes through the village. The Post Office, on the left, was demolished during the early 1950s. The postmaster during the early 1900s was Fred Gardner and letters arrived at 7 a.m. and 3 p.m.

Warehead. The track to the left leads to Halnaker Windmill and is a continuation of Stane Street. The miller's house adjoins the track in the background.

Duchess Cottages at Redvins. During the second half of the 19th century the sixth Duke of Richmond, anxious to improve the welfare of his tenants, built on the Goodwood Estate 49 distinctive pairs of flint cottages, some as far afield as Felpham. Thirty-six of these were constructed in the style of an 'H' plan and contained three bedrooms, a workroom/kitchen, living room and pantry; in addition, each pair had a separate outhouse containing woodsheds, privies and communal wash-house with oven and copper. The origin of the term 'Duchess Cottage' is uncertain, although it probably relates to the interest the sixth Duchess of Richmond expressed in their design.

Mr McCarthy, the village carrier, with his Ford van. He ran a weekly delivery and collection service to Chichester.

Mr and Mrs McCarthy standing by their pigsty. Almost every cottager kept pigs, which provided the family with its main supply of meat as well as an extra source of income.

Upwaltham. The 12th-century church of St Mary the Virgin, photographed early this century, is a fine example of a small Downland church retaining its original plan. It is one of only four Sussex churches with a rounded chancel. During the 1970s a chapel of similar size and design was excavated at Chilgrove. Upwaltham is a tiny parish and hamlet at the head of the Upper Lavant Valley.

Tangmere. A quiet village scene early this century before Tangmere became the famous Royal Air Force fighter base in the Second World War.

Strettington. A view from the Goodwood road looking towards Strettington House.

Westerton. It was no more than a hamlet at the turn of the century, consisting of the farm and a few cottages.

affham Post Office

Graffham. The Post Office c. 1908. It was established in 1746 and owned by the Pescod family until the early 1960s.

A village scene early this century. The man is the Revd Arthur Newman, whose half plate camera took many of the photographs in this book.

The Revd Newman's brother was vicar of Bignor and Sutton. He is seen visiting a parishioner.

The village shop. The gentleman in the doorway is the proprietor, Jesse Gumbrell.

The village shop today, now converted into a private house.

The Mill. The building carries the date 1844. It had become a private house by the 1930s. At the time of the Domesday Book there were two mills recorded at Bignor.

SECTION FOUR

Medicine

During the second half of the 19th century Singleton had a resident doctor, Dr Turner, who was succeeded in 1886 by Dr Harry Harlock. He moved his growing practice in 1902 to Summersdale Lodge and after his death in 1905 his successor Dr Garratt acquired No. 8 Lavant Road, where the Practice is still based today.

There were a Doctor's Club and the Foresters' and Friendly Societies into which villagers could pay a regular subscription to ensure medical attention when needed. However, Dr Harlock is known to have done much of his work for nothing. In addition a Nursing Fund was established to provide trained nursing care for patients at home.

Childbirth took place at home and some village women could take over the role of midwife in the absence of the doctor or district nurse. They would also for 2s 6d provide a 'nine day service' looking after the home, while the mother regained her strength.

There were many home remedies, such as adder fat for rheumatism and the squeezing of a baked onion into the ear for ear-ache.

Dr Harry Harlock M.R.C.S., L.R.C.P., Doctor to the villages in the Upper Lavant Valley from 1886–1905. He qualified from University College, London in 1884. Originating from Ely, he came to Singleton after serving as a house surgeon to the Brecon County Infirmary. After his premature death from pneumonia he was much mourned by his patients. His obituary in the Singleton Parish Magazine records that 'he was a true friend of the people of the parish who never spared himself but worked night and day and wore himself out in the service of others.'

Dr Harlock's gig with Jim Crocker, his groom and general handyman.

Little Drove House, Dr Harlock's home and surgery in Singleton. The Harlocks employed a cook, parlour maid, governess, nursemaid and a young boy called 'Buttons.' They had three sons and a daughter.

Summersdale Lodge. The house was built in 1902 for Dr Harlock as a home and surgery with financial help from Mr Willie James in grateful recognition for curing his daughter, Millicent, of diphtheria. Between the wars it became a boys' Preparatory School and was demolished in the early 1960s.

Dr. Wilfrid Coltart carving Christmas dinner at the Royal West Sussex Hospital. Dr Coltart joined the Lavant Road practice in 1934 as partner to Dr Bulstrode. He retired as Senior Partner in 1978. Work as a country doctor before and during the War was hard, especially when Dr Coltart had no partner. Morning surgery was from 8.45 a.m. until 10.15 a.m. He made his visits throughout the day before evening surgery at 6 p.m. which would last until 8 p.m. Night calls were frequent and, in addition to his general practice work, he gave anaesthetics twice a week at the hospital.

The Chichester Infirmary, built in 1826. The foundation stone had been laid by the Duke of Richmond a year earlier. It made medical history by being the first hospital in England to use the stethoscope, which was introduced by the Infirmary's Honorary Physician, John Forbes. The Infirmary was funded by public subscription, and among its benefactors was Mr Willie James of West Dean. King George V renamed the Infirmary The Royal West Sussex Hospital in 1913 in memory of his father, Edward VII.

Nursing staff on the lawn at Chichester Infirmary, about 1912. There has been a tennis tournament for the nurses, with prizes, which include a Brownie box camera. On the right, behind the open photograph album, Matron is sitting with the Home sister beside her. Only fully trained staff were allowed to wear white caps.

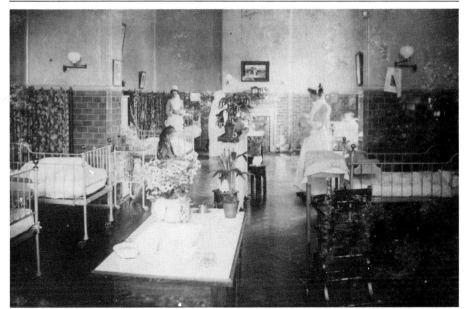

Children's ward in Chichester Infirmary, about 1913. A nursing sister is on the left and Matron on the right.

You may wonder why a framed enlargement of this old photo of Scottish Black-face sheep is hanging in a West Dean farm house. The prize ram was sold at Perth for £90 in 1889. Thanks to this sale and a timely inheritance, a young Scottish student was able to go to the London Polytechnic and later to St Mary's Hospital, London University. He became the Nobel prizewinner, Sir Alexander Fleming, the discoverer of penicillin.

Retirement presentation to Nurse Selina Harding, District nurse at Singleton from 1919–1956. She was the first District nurse to be awarded the MBE. Also in the picture: Mrs Betty O'Hagan, Mrs Davies, headmistress of the school, Ted Court of Singleton Stores, Fred Uden of the Post Office, Bill Smith, Maurice Hill and Glenys Freemantle. Nurse Harding was a wise and devoted friend to all her patients. Working closely with the doctors, she also had some favourite remedies of her own, e.g. ginger beer for nearly all stomach disorders.

SECTION FIVE

The Railway

The Chichester to Midhurst line was opened in 1881 by the London, Brighton and South Coast Railway Company. It closed to passenger traffic in 1935, although a goods service was maintained until 1956, when the track between Lavant and Cocking was taken up. The line between Lavant and Chichester continued to be used during the late 1950s and early 1960s to carry sugar beet from local farms. The railway played an important part in the life of the Upper Lavant Valley villages. Most of the provisions went by rail, so did the output of Charlton Sawmill – brush and broom backs, handles for knives, dowels and other products. Milk floats with churns from neighbouring farms usually caught the 9 a.m. train. If they were late there would be a last desperate gallop up Station Hill into the Singleton goods yard.

Villagers would often tell the time by the trains. The daily papers arrived by 9.00 a.m. when there were two trains in the station at the same time, the 'up train' going on to Victoria. The return fare from Singleton to Chichester was 11d. Singleton, for a country station, was to experience many memorable occasions between its opening and 1914 through the association with Goodwood Races and the regular visits of royalty to West Dean House. Today the Stationmaster's house is the home of the Paget family, who run the Chilsdown Vineyard. The former booking office is now the winery.

The railway navvies at Singleton, c. 1880. They were a wild, hard-working, hard-drinking lot, and were occasionally brought before magistrates charged with being drunk or even, in one case, 'smashing a quart pot against a policeman's head.' The locomotive is a contractor's engine named Fred.

Navvies outside Singleton Station, probably taken at the same time as the previous photograph. While the Stationmaster's house is nearing completion, the canopies to the station platforms and the covered way to the subway still remain to be built.

Class B4 No. 60 Kimberley at Singleton with the Royal Train. The journey from Victoria via Dorking, Horsham, Pulborough, Petworth and Midhurst, took one hour and forty-five minutes. For the King's arrival the platform was covered in a red carpet. He would be met by Mr Willie James who accompanied him on the short journey to West Dean. When visiting Goodwood House, the King would travel to Drayton Station, a small halt between Chichester and Barnham.

Unloading horse boxes was once a familiar sight at Singleton and Lavant Stations.

Singleton Station looking south towards West Dean during the early 1930s. The water tower is on the left and the signal box on the right. During the Second World War, Lord Haw Haw mentioned in a broadcast that the tunnels at Singleton and Cocking were being used to store ammunition. This may have been why the Germans dropped bombs nearby, though not quite on target at Cucumber Farm.

Singleton Station looking north, during the early 1930s.

Singleton Station with two trains and what are probably horse boxes in the siding to the right of the picture. The letters SPL, just visible, suggest that the engine on the right was a Special for race week.

Cocking Station in 1881 shortly after the opening of the line. Henry Chapman, the first Stationmaster, is standing on the platform. The Stationmaster's pay was £1 8s per week. Today the Station house has been magnificently restored as a private home.

Lavant Station in 1881. George Harmer, the first Stationmaster, stands outside. The Station too played an important role during race week, when extra staff were taken on to cope with the additional traffic and there was no space for horse boxes at Singleton. The Station's future is still undecided. Current plans include conversion to flats and a possible restoration of the line for recreational use.

SECTION SIX

Agriculture and Woodland Crafts

Agriculture, forestry and the crafts associated with them were the main sources of employment. At the turn of the century, for example, the labour force at Charlton Farm consisted of eighteen men, while Charles Pitt at Newhouse Farm, East Dean, employed three threshing gangs. It is interesting to note that Charlton Farm is now part of the Goodwood Estate Home Farm, and its buildings are the Weald and Downland Open Air Museum's workshops and stores.

Sheep and arable farming suited the local environment and until the First World War every farm in the area had a flock of Southdown Sheep. The breed had been developed by John Ellman of Glynde in East Sussex during the late 18th century. It created much interest amongst the aristocracy, including the Dukes of Richmond. During race week the sixth Duke paraded his flock in front of the House every morning. The Downs provided excellent grazing and the sheep helped to prevent scrub from growing hence the 'springy' downland turf. In addition by folding the sheep in winter on root crops, they ensured a well manured field for the growing corn. The average size of a folding flock was between 250 and 400 sheep.

The breed was famous for the quality of its mutton and wool, but the need to plough the Downs during the two World Wars and the increasing desire amongst farmers to have larger breeds meant that the number of Southdown flocks were considerably reduced to make it almost an endangered breed.

The villages in the Upper Lavant Valley were surrounded by large areas of woodland, dominated by Charlton Forest. It was therefore natural that many villagers should find employment in woodland industries, notably in East Dean, where there were seven hurdle-makers. Other local crafts included making thatching spars, chair legs, barrel hoops and cleft chestnut paling; tennis racquets were made from ash. Surplus wood was used for mast stops, barrel hoops and sheep troughs. The coppice could be bought as it stood at the annual underwood sale at the Richmond Arms, Goodwood. The underwood merchants at East Dean were Henry Wild, Henry West and the Kennett Brothers.

Shepherd Turner of Westmeston. Mr Turner's clothing is perhaps typical of the Downland shepherd early this century. The wintry scene shows that the photograph is taken in a lambing fold. To keep out the cold Mr Turner is wearing a great coat and cape made of calico or canvas waterproofed in boiled oil. His hat, which may have been made out of dog hair, would have been particularly hard to prevent denting. He stands sentinel with his 'Bobtail' Sussex sheepdog and crook in hand. A wattle feeding cage is on his left.

Shepherd Ruddock in the sheepfold at East Dean. The hurdle makers made long cages of ashwood for the sheep to feed from, or circular ones made from hazel.

Sheep washing at Merston. A typical country scene during the early part of the century. Both Lavant and Singleton had sheep washes in the River Lavant. The sheep would be penned before being released to be scrubbed and dipped, as the photographs show. They would then be released into the mainstream to swim down river until they could scramble out and shake themselves dry. It is interesting to note that the Caryll family, who once owned the Manor of Merston, were the previous owners of Goodwood during the 17th century. The third Duke of Richmond also once owned farmland in Merston.

Bill Taylor, born at West Dean and shepherd at Binderton for over 40 years. As a boy he remembers seeing King Edward VII at shooting party lunches. Young Bill received medals and a clock from Mr Willie James for good attendance at West Dean School. The James family were good landlords, and each year every child at the school would receive a new pair of shoes from a London shoemaker, who made a special visit to the school. Mr Taylor is seen here outside his 19th century shepherds' hut or van, which needed four horses to transport it. His dog is a cross between a collie and an old English sheepdog. The collie breed was introduced to the area by the Dukes of Richmond from their Scottish Estates and first used on the Goodwood Farms.

Horace Oliver hand-shearing a Southdown. Between 40 and 50 sheep a day could be hand-shorn – electric shears would do twice as many in the time. Shearing would normally be undertaken by 'Gangs' and one of seven from Sidlesham operated in the area. It was thirsty work and large quantities of beer were drunk throughout the day, culminating on the last night of the season with a celebration known as 'Black Ram Night'.

Although in his mid 80s, Mr Oliver still works at Newhouse Farm, East Dean, where he tends the only pedigree flock of Southdowns now in the area. Coming from three generations of shepherds, he had seven brothers and four sisters. In a small cottage with two rooms upstairs and two downstairs, his father raised the family on a weekly wage of 15s.

When he left school at twelve years old Horace became a shepherd's boy, working with his father on a farm at Burpham, near Arundel. He would regularly drive sheep to markets at Barnham and Chichester. For the annual Findon Fair they had to start at 2 a.m. to get there by 6 a.m.

George Penny shearing a Dorset ewe at Hill Top, Cucumber Farm, Singleton.

Probably Charlie Smith, ploughing on Cucumber Farm, c.1900. Note the low coulter and the size of the horses, which are small in comparison with the plough.

John Farley ploughing at Wolverstone Farm. The farm had four horses and Mr Farley refused ever to use a tractor. He called it a 'Paraffin Race Horse.'

A Sussex wagon at Bignor, c. 1910. The body was painted blue and the wheels red. The box and wheel falloes were made of elm and the spokes of ash. With its small turning circle it was awkward to turn. A skid pad was attached for braking a rear wheel on slopes.

William Farley, with his two horses, probably Blossom and Violet, mowing hay at Wolverstone Farm.

Building a hay rick at Chilgrove. The horse on the left is working the elevator turning a portable 'gin.'

'Old Joe' Coles on the Sussex wagon, harvesting at Upwaltham Farm.

Amos Hall and his wife Maggie thatching a corn rick on the Goodwood Estate. Maggie is carrying a sheaf on a 'dog', which was a fork made of chestnut or hazel and carried on her back up the ladder.

John Chapman cultivating with a 1927 Fordson, the first tractor at Upwaltham Farm. The Chapman brothers, John, Philip and Greg with their father Charles were tenants of the 1000 acre farm from the Petworth Estate in 1927 sharing the responsibility between them. Greg managed the flock of Southdowns and Phil the other livestock, starting with a small herd of shorthorns and some pigs. John looked after the arable.

Mrs Farley, with possibly William Farley, milking outside the cowshed at Wolverstone Farm. The advertisement says 'Pink's mineral waters and fruit crushes, the finest on the south coast.'

Newhouse Farm, East Dean, formerly Stein Farm – 'Stein' meaning stone. Stone picking was once a regular source of employment for village women and children. The flints were put into a bucket and in turn emptied into a square box, one cubic yard in size. One shilling was paid for each cubic yard picked. The flints were used in building work and road making.

The farmhouse is architecturally very interesting, although little is known about its history. It was probably built during the second half of the 18th century as a shooting or hunting box.

Mr Jupp, charcoal burner, in Charlton Forest. In front of him are his dixie for cooking and two buckets used for dousing the kiln. He would live in his hut for twelve to fourteen months, until the cordwood ran out, when he moved on to another site. His friend Mr Davies transported the charcoal to Singleton Station by horse and cart. Mr Jupp is reported to have been violently sick every Monday morning from the constant breathing of charcoal fumes.

Mr and Mrs Arthur Langridge, two retired charcoal burners, constructing a hut at the Weald and Downland Open Air Museum. The pole frame is about ten ft. across and the hut would be made with an inner lining of sacking, re-inforced on top with a layer of twigs, with leaves and then turf stacked horizontally.

Mr Arthur Langridge tending a smoking earth kiln with a 'rauber' during a charcoal burn at the Weald and Downland Open Air Museum. For centuries charcoal burning was a familiar sight in Sussex, but by the Second World War for social and economic reasons it had become a dying woodland industry. The traditional method using an earth kiln took approximately three days and two nights to burn, and a six cord kiln could produce about one and a half tons of charcoal.

Charcoal burning with metal kilns was revived during the 1930s and 1940s in Charlton Forest and at Charlton Sawmill by the Sussex Charcoal Burning Company. The charcoal produced during the war was used for industrial purposes and also for gas masks.

Charlton Sawmill c.1889. It had been opened in 1863 and for many years was one of the main sources of employment for Singleton, Charlton and East Dean. During the late 19th century it was managed by Foster and Foster. The family lived in Fox Hall. Note the 'jigger' wheels in the centre of the picture, used for dragging timber out of the woods.

Charlton Sawmill early in the century. In the shed on the left there is a rack-saw for cutting timber. The two chimneys are for the steam engines driving the circular saw in the tall mill. On the far right ash cut into lengths is stacked for drying. It was used, as it still is today, for handles and the making of cricket stumps. Smaller sections of beech were stacked in a similar way, for conversion to dowels used in the furniture trade.

A sawyer, employed at Charlton Sawmill c.1889. He is holding a six ft. peg tooth crosscut saw that was used for cutting or 'bucking' a felled tree into lengths before loading on to a wagon. He would also appear to be wearing an additional pair of trousers which must have borne some significance for his work. The criss-cross fencing was the kind often used to mark cottage garden boundaries.

Foresters with horses, collecting timber from woods near Cocking Causeway c.1916.

Henry Wild spar-making on the Goodwood Estate during the early 1900s. Spars were used for thatching and made from coppiced hazel. They were made two ft. three in. in length for roofs, three ft. for hay ricks and four ft. six in. for corn ricks. The length of those in the picture shows that they were probably being made for a corn rick. Henry Wild was one of the East Dean underwood merchants and supplied a variety of coppice products, including hurdles, sheep cages, spars, hoops, clothes props, faggots, pea boughs, bean sticks, stakes and firewood.

Albert Peacock spar-making at the Weald and Downland Open Air Museum. The canvas shelter gives protection from the sun and rain. Albert's father was a timber-thrower and the family lived at Buriton Farm on the West Dean Estate. The second eldest of a family of ten children, Albert learnt to split hazel at the age of nine, a task he used to do before walking the three miles to school. After spending most of his life working in agriculture, he now demonstrates spar-making at the Museum, producing 5,000 a week.

Ernie Austin of East Dean splitting hazel for wattling a hurdle. The craft traditionally required a five year apprenticeship and boys would start at the age of 12 to learn it. About nine acres of hazel were needed in a year to produce 3,600 hurdles (400 to the acre). Hurdles for Southdown sheep were two ft. nine in. high, while those for Dorset or Hampshire Downs were three ft. It was possible to make a dozen hurdles a day. Prices varied from 3s 6d a dozen before the First World War to 10s. a dozen after it. The price today would be £96 a dozen.

Bill Gumbleton of East Dean with a finished wattle hurdle.

The Weald & Downland Open Air Museum

by Roy Armstrong, Museum Founder

In 1967 a Committee which had been convened for the Promotion of an Open Air Museum for the Weald approached the Educational Foundation which Mr Edward James had recently set up based on his 6000 acres of the West Dean Estate. The idea interested him and a number of possible sites on the Estate were suggested by his Agent.

The site most favoured by the Committee lay on both sides of the River Lavant, south of West Dean House and close to the village of West Dean. This site, however, was understandably not welcomed by the residents of the village, and Edward James himself suggested that the large field in the parish of Singleton which was used for annual sheep-dog trials might be considered. The Committee agreed that, combined with the surrounding woodland, it would be suitable and the Foundation agreed to the lease of the site to the Museum at the nominal peppercorn rental.

Since the whole of the Downland had been designated as 'An Area of Outstanding Natural Beauty', even though conservation was a principal aim of the Museum, building was rightly regarded as questionable. The problem of access was also difficult to resolve, so that negotiations with the Planning Authority dragged on for over a year.

In the meantime it was possible to accept the offer of two medieval farmhouses from Bough Beech, destined for demolition from a reservoir site on the Sussex/Kent border. The Foundation offered storage space in the railway cutting north of Singleton Station, and transport of the dismantled materials.

A Toll Cottage, damaged by a lorry at Upper Beeding, was also offered to the Museum, and a Treadwheel for raising water from a deep well at Catherington in

East Hants. Both were collected and put into store.

At this time John Lowe, the Director of Birmingham City Museum, agreed to become Honorary Director of the Museum on a part time basis for two years.

Well-wishers of the Museum gave substantial practical help – especially those with special skills in building and surveying, so that as soon as planning permission was granted it became possible to start a number of projects. Two of these – the repair and re-erection of the Toll Cottage, and the setting up of a Charcoal Burner's site, were carried through entirely by volunteers. The Museum was very fortunate in making contact with Mr and Mrs Langridge, living at Kingsfold on the Surrey border, retired charcoal burners who still remembered the traditional methods and life-style of the craft. They supervised and virtually built the original charcoal burner's hut and demonstration kilns.

The Museum's first considerable building was Winkhurst Farmhouse – the smaller of the two houses from the Bough Beech Reservoir. On 3 March 1969 a temporary workshop was set up and on 1 April the whole of the frame of Winkhurst was re-erected by Gunholt Greiner and Roger Champion.

During that summer Roger Champion carried out the repair of the Treadwheel using the protective shelter of Winkhurst as a workshop.

It was decided that in the autumn of 1970 there should be an opening of the site to visitors for six consecutive weekends, the purpose being to explain what was intended. The response exceeded all expectations, and it was agreed that the Museum should open regularly at weekends after Easter of the following year.

The planning of the site has been complicated as it formed part of a scheme of large scale landscape gardening carried out in the 18th and 19th centuries.

The woodlands had been carefully planted and defined, with characteristic clumping, according to the ideas dominant at that time. This landscape had little relationship to the earlier land use and landscape to which most of the buildings in the Museum were related. From the start some landscaping of the site was necessary; even before the trial opening of the Museum in the autumn of 1970 extensive tree planting on the eastern edge, to provide a screen to the proposed access and car-parking areas was undertaken, and in the north-east corner a pond was dug, later to be deepened and extended when the Lurgashall Mill was erected.

Siting the Museum at Singleton, right in the chalk area, had involved widening the scope of the Museum in its catchment area and the type of buildings to be re-erected. An 'Open Air Museum for the Weald' became 'An Open Air Museum for the Weald and Downland'.

In the last fifteen years as many buildings have been given to the Museum from the chalk area as from the Weald – to name a few, Titchfield Market Hall, the Court barn and the Chilcomb Granary from East Hants, and the North Cray House and the aisled hall from Sole Street from the chalk area of North Kent.

In all this, the Edward James Foundation has been continuously generous and helpful, and the Museum site itself since 1970 has been extended and developed from 35 acres to its present size of approximately 60 acres.

The Museum has become very much part of the local community. A redundant complex of farm buildings at Charlton, leased from the Goodwood Estate, has been converted to provide stores and workshops. The management of a 20 acre area of historic woodland, also leased from Goodwood, has been undertaken.

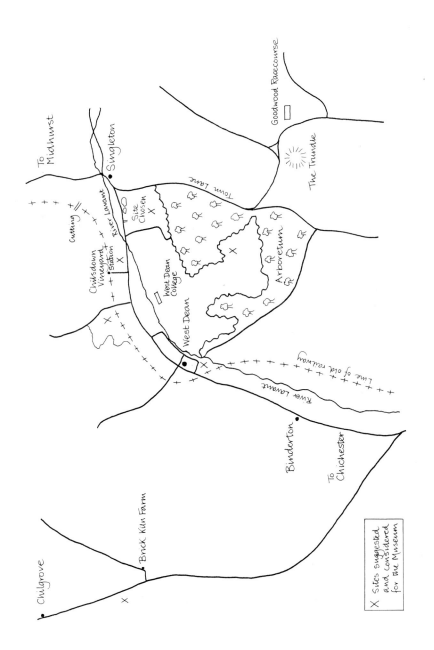

The Museum site about 1968, before work started. For a number of years the West Sussex Young Farmers held their annual sheep dog trials here.

A similar view today.

The re-erection of Winkhurst during 1969. This medieval timber-framed house from the site of the Bough Beech reservoir, Kent, was the first building to be re-erected at the Museum.

The timber-frame and bricks of the early 17th-century Catherington Treadwheel awaiting reconstruction. In the background work is being carried out on the Upper Beeding Toll Cottage. Volunteer workers' tents are on the right.

The Upper Beeding Toll Cottage and entrance sign in 1970, when the Museum first opened.

The Lower Mill Pond under excavation and the Blacksmith's Forge from Southwater, near Horsham. During the excavations the remains of a Roman building were discovered in the area to the right of the picture.

Volunteers working on the reconstruction of the small cottage from Hangleton. It is based on two buildings excavated during the 1950s on the site of the deserted medieval village of Hangleton, near Hove. Eric Holden, who supervised the reconstruction, is seen (second from left of cement mixer). During the 1970s the remains of a deserted medieval village were found at Monkton on the West Dean Estate.

'Bayleaf' Farmhouse, a fine example of a 15th-century Wealden house from Bough Beech under reconstruction during the summer of 1971. Dismantled in 1968, it was the third house to be presented to the Museum by the East Surrey Water Company.

Chris Zeuner and Roger Champion working on the reconstruction of Bayleaf with a volunteer, Peter Parish – and a part of somebody else?

REFERENCES AND FURTHER READING

Three Medieval Sites in West Dean Parish by F. Aldsworth (Sussex Archaeological Collections 1978)
Woodcolliers and Charcoal Burners by L. Armstrong (Coach Publishing House Ltd 1978)
The Chichester and Midhurst Railway by P. Clark (Turn Table Publications 1979)
Domesday Book, Sussex, edited by John Morris (Phillimore 1976)
Dallaway's *Western Sussex* Vol. 2, 1815.
The Edward James Foundation edited by N. Simon (Edward James Foundation 1981)
Notes on Monkton House (Edward James Foundation)
Shepherds of Britain by A. Gosset (Constable and Co. 1911)
The Family Fortune by Alan Hill (Scan Books 1978)
Nature in Downland by W.H. Hudson (J.M. Dent & Sons Ltd 1923)
Goodwood Estate Archives
Goodwood by David Hunn (Davies-Poynter 1975)
Kelly's Directories
Downland Farming at Upwaltham Farm 1927–1939 by Barbara Laming (West Sussex   History Journal, Sept.
    1984)
Buildings connected with the Charlton Hunt (Landmark Trust)
King Edward VII by Philip Magnus (John Murray 1964)
Records of the Old Charlton Hunt by the Earl of March (1910)
History of Midhurst by the Midhurst Exhibitions Project Team (1984)
Track Back by Elizabeth Newbery (Weald and Downland Open Air Museum 1986)
The Fast Set by G. Plumptre (Andre-Deutsch 1984)
Sussex, People, Places, Things by Bernard Price (Phillimore 1975)
Guide to Boxgrove Priory by R. Ratcliff
Singleton Parish Magazines (1895–1905)
Our Villages within Living Memory by the late Mrs M. Bury and Singleton and East Dean W.I. (1958)
Branch Lines to Midhurst by K. Smith and V. Mitchell (Middleton Press 1981)
The Southdown Sheep (Southdown Sheep Society 1933)
Halnaker in Sussex by Francis W. Steer (1958)
Royal West Sussex Hospital 1774–1884 by Francis W. Steer (Chichester Papers 1960)
Guide to Upwaltham Church by Francis W. Steer (Sussex Historic Churches Trust)
Sussex People, Places, Things by Bernard Price (Phillimore 1975)
Sussex Smugglers (W.J. Smith, Brighton)
West Dean Estate Archives
West Dean Rabbit Warren by R. and A. Tittensor (1986)
The Royal Family by Pen and Camera by S.A. Tooley (Cassell and Co. Ltd. 1907)
The Country House Remembered edited by M. Waterson (Routledge and Kegan Paul 1985)
Weald and Downland Open Air Museum Guide Books
West Sussex County Record Office. Taped interview with Mr W. Taylor (ref. W.S.R.O. OH16)
West Sussex Gazette and Chichester Observer Archives
Wisden Cricketers' Almanacks (John Wisden & Co. Ltd)

ACKNOWLEDGEMENTS

We would like to thank the very many people who have helped us in the compilation of this book by lending photographs or providing information. We are most grateful to the following for their generous assistance:

Miss L. Adams, Mr and Mrs J.R. Armstrong, Mrs G. Atkinson, Mr T. Austin, Mr J. Aylwin, Mr G. Bevis, Revd J. Bishop, the late Mrs M. Bury and Singleton and East Dean Women's Institute, the late Mr M. Carter, Mr R. Champion, Mr and Mrs J. Chapman, Mrs P. Clery, Dr W. Coltart, Misses A. and R. Crees, Miss K. Crook, Mrs P. Davies, Mr R. Fabricius, Miss A. Farley, the late Mr J. Farley, Mr W. Fleming, The Trustees of the Goodwood Collections, Brigadier W. Greenway, Mrs M. Hall, Mrs J. Hampton, Mr T. Harcombe, Mr E. Harlock, Mr R. Harmer, Miss S. Hart, Mrs J. Herrington, Mr M. Heymann, Mr I. Hicks, Mr J. Holt, Mr J. Howick, Mr D. Humphrey, Mr R. Hunt, The Trustees of the Edward James Foundation, Mr L. Jasper, Mr W. Jupp, Mrs N. Laishley, The Landmark Trust, Mr W. Langmead, Mr D. Legg-Willis, Mr K. Leslie, Mr A. Lillywhite, Mr A. Long, Mr G. Long, the Earl of March, Mr W. Mitchell, Mr M T. McCann, Mrs O. Merry, National Motor Museum, Beaulieu, Miss N. Newman, Mrs C. Nicoll, Mr H. Oliver, Dr D.B. Pailthorpe, Mr A. Peacock, Mr G. Plumptre, Mr H. Potter, Mr C. Pratt, Mr B. Price, Revd M. Reeve, The Duke of Richmond and Gordon, Mr K. Smith, Miss V. Smith, The Royal College of Surgeons, Mrs D. Taylor, the late Mr W. Taylor, Mr and Mrs A. Turnbull, Mrs M. Turner, Mr D. Wallis, Mr C. Wells, Mrs I. West, Mr L. West, West Sussex County Record Office and County Archivist, Mr and Mrs A. Wilkins, Mrs M. Woods, Mr A. Wright, Mrs J. Young, Mr C. Zeuner.

And our warm thanks to our wives Jane and Anne for infinite patience and much hard work.

PHOTOGRAPH CREDITS

J. Butwin 98, Country Life 35a, East Sussex County Library 54b, Executors of the late T. Edmondson 144, Trustees of the Edward James Foundation 30, 31a, b, 32, 33, 34b, 38, Trustees of the Goodwood Collection 22, 23, 27a, 73, W. Jupp 149, Lens of Sutton 125b, The Mansell Collection 130, National Photographic Society. Front Cover, Portsmouth and Sunderland Newspapers p.l.c. 28, 118b, 122, 136a, W.W. Rouch and Co 17b, 20a, 20b, 21a, 126a, Sussex Police Archives 17a, West Sussex County Library 40b, 50a, b, 51, 52b, 69, 105, 128a, b, West Sussex County Record Office 2 (PH 9437), 21b (PH 3332), 26a (PH 24), 99a (PH18), The Armstrong Library, Weald and Downland Open Air Museum 143, 154a, 155, 156, 157b, 158, The late E. Wallis Collection 124, 125a, Mrs M. Woods 138, 140a.